You Are Enough:

*The Branding Guide for
Accelerating Your Expertise.*

By: Shade' Y Adu

You Have What It Takes

First thing you need to know is that you have what it takes to be successful. You have been trained. You have the ingredients. You may just not have put them together. Maybe you haven't been giving the recipe yet, but the ingredients are there ready to put together because you are enough.

I know what this is like, I was a teacher. I had been trained as an educator, I knew how to educate people as a teacher but I was scared to be a branding expert. Even though I had done it, I was afraid to step out and call myself.

I was afraid because I didn't have a degree in branding or marketing. I came from a background where: You got the certification; You got the degree; That is how people knew that you were an expert.

I was afraid of that transition of going from educator to entrepreneur because I didn't want people to see me as a pretender. I wanted them to see me as an expert.

I used to just lean on what I was doing in the past because of insecurity. I was extremely afraid and nervous about claiming to be an expert in a field that I had no formal training in.

What I actually was finding, was that I felt like I had

become a novice overnight. I had gone from expert in my field to beginner. Now you need to know that this was more how I was feeling about it, then necessarily what was true. Because the first thing that I had to do was believe in myself, the rest came from stepping out and knowing that I was enough.

One day, I realized that in my life God had been preparing me to step into entrepreneurship and help women entrepreneurs with their branding

So I hired a coach that helped to mentor me and the very first thing that that coach told me was, "**You are enough**." They helped me see that all the experiences that I had had in life, had been preparing me to be a branding expert. I already had easy answers. I just needed to be able to give them out.

I had to believe it was possible.

Beginning to Realize

As I began to work with people, I began to see that the questions that they were asking me, I had the answers for. And I began to release within myself that belief that I am enough. "I know how to do this," I said to myself. It was there the whole time, all I needed to do was just put myself in a situation so that it could be brought out.

A man contacted me for help. As I just started to talk to him I realized that the help that he needed was with his brand. I told him what he needed to do. I showed him that he just needed to do it.

As I helped him I realized that what I was actually doing was branding him. I realized in that moment that I was enough.

It actually happened from putting myself out there and just actually doing it.

In the doing I realized, "Hey, this is not that difficult. I actually do know how to do what I thought I didn't know how to do."

But you just have to start. You have to be willing to try it. When I stepped out is when the lightbulb kind of went off as if to say, "Okay, I can do this. I have been prepared. I am actually enough to do it, because I am doing it."

I've realized that it was there the whole time. It just needed to be more visible and brought out.

Being Seen

So now what I do is I help people break out of their shells, so that they can be seen. This is why branding is so exciting to me. It helps people who are hidden in the shadows really be seen as the expert as what they are.

Not all of us are Oprah, but all of us do have the ability to be the expert at what we are here for. Once you step out of the shadows and are visible, then you can be heard. The message that you've been given can be heard by the world. Because in order to be heard, people need to see you.

Visibility is huge.

I love helping people break out of their shell and be seen. A lot of times, the women that I work with, they are afraid to be heard and they are afraid to be seen. And because of that, it hinders their profits.

If people don't know you, if they don't like you and they don't trust you and they can't see you, they don't know you exist. They cannot purchase your programs, products and services

That is why we position ourselves an expert. So that we can be seen for one reason, and that is to serve others.

Serving Others

I know the people that I help are serving someone. They are solving a problem that every night someone is Googling trying to find the answer to. There up people that can't sleep because they need your service. But they can't because you haven't established yourself

So we need to #1; know that we are enough. Know that if

we are seen, especially by our target audience, that will help us be able to serve.

You can't be the entrepreneur rock star that you want to be because no one knows that you exist. Not establishing yourself as an expert, keeps you the best kept secret in your niche and it keeps you unprofitable.

In order to really truly be successful in business, everyone does not need to know that you exist, but your target audience needs to know that you exist.

They need to know that you are talking to them. They need to know that you are there for them. They need to know you. They are looking for you; they just can't find you right now. Because you haven't established yourself as someone who can help.

Passion, Purpose & Profit

We can serve our target audience and then let them know we can help them and that we are here to serve them. This is when we come to the place where we have an alignment of passion, purpose and profits.

Passion is what you love to do. Its doing that thing that you were born to do, that you were created for, that keeps you up all night. That is your passion.

Your purpose is that thing that you were born into. It is inside of you. You are here for a reason and that is your purpose.

And then of course profit is just simply that you are making enough money. It is knowing that what you are doing can continue on to be done.

That's what I call my greatness branding, the alignment of purpose, passion and profit.

I compare it a lot to a car. The car is your passion, the steering wheel is your purpose, because it tells you where to go, and your profits are your fuel. So if you want that car to go, you need to put gas in the tank.

You can have passion, you can have a purpose, but if it's not profitable—

That's really one of those major pains that a lot of women that come to me have, if you can't fuel that gas tank, there is only so far you can go.

An Expert

The thing is a lot of us shy away of the concept of expertise. Of calling ourselves an expert, but the truth is we pay attention to experts. Experts are people who are easily recognizable and experts get paid more money. You can expedite that and accelerate your profits and your expertise by positioning yourself as an expert.

Think about it, if you go to a specialist, like say for example if you have a heart problem, you want to go to a cardiologist. You want somebody who specializes in working on your heart. You want to go to a heart doctor, not just a general practitioner that is going to tell you have got a problem with your heart. You want to go to a guy that is going to tell you, this is how you are going to solve the problem with your heart.

An expert provides clarity. A very clear and recognizable solution. If you are trying to solve too many problems, you really are solving no problem.

So you really want to speak to a specific pain point or a specific issue for a specific group. That is where we create a thing called clarity. By being specific we save the market from confusion. The biggest thing we don't want to do is confuse our market. Because when we confuse our market it hinders our profitable. And the truth is the confusion causes us to serve no one.

Specializing=Visible

When we embrace the fact that being talented in one area is enough, then we can be an expert in that area. When we give in to the feeling that says, "Being an expert in one area will limiting our ability to serve", we actually experience just the opposite.

When we try to serve everyone, we are creating confusion in the marketplace.

In actuality we are serving no one.

It's really scary for a lot of people, especially when an entrepreneur says, "I can do this and I can do that." The multitalented visionary. I call it the visionary syndrome. They want to do everything because they have a lot of talent. But in actuality, they need to understand that just being talented and wise in one area is enough.

By not specializing no one knows what we do and we

actually miss out on serving the people that we are put here to serve in the first place.

When we stand out we become visible. When we become clear and specific, we become seen. We look at it from a lack and a deficit that we are not going to have enough if we limit ourselves to one particular field or niche market. When in actuality it's the opposite. We make ourselves stand out more. WE allow ourselves to become more visible in the marketplace because we do that one particular thing and we do it extremely well. Versus everyone else who is trying to be a generalist.

When you have someone for example who is a health coach to post-partum mothers, we know specifically who to send to them. We know that if I'm just having a baby and I want to get back in shape, this is my coach because he or she is going to specifically talk to the needs of what I need after just giving birth.

Most successful companies have a very particular market. A perfect example of that would be Amazon. Amazon spent years just selling books. Now they sell a whole lot of other things, but they became experts at selling and delivering books. That's what they did first. We can always expand to more things, but it has to start from the specific.

Jeff Bezos, the CEO and founder of Amazon.com says, "Branding is not what you say, it's what other people say when you are not in the room."

Ease and grace comes from branding yourself as that expert, when you are clear people will do your promoting for you. Because keep in mind your brand isn't about you, it's about the people you serve. If we are not stepping out in that confidence, we literally are becoming invisible because the market can't find us. There are people that are actually literally looking for what we are doing and they can't find the help that they need because you have what they need and they can't see you.

An Expensive Hobby

What embracing my gifting for branding really meant in my life is, that I had to come to terms with the fact that I had to either brand myself, educate myself, and really step out as a branding specialist, or I had to acknowledge that I was just running a very expensive hobby.

I decided that it was time to take myself as my first customer. I needed to rebrand myself as a brand strategist and not just keep telling people I was an educator.

The question I have for you is how broke do you need to get before you believe in yourself, brand yourself and then get to work? You have to get uncomfortable enough to get you out of your comfort.

Lack of self-confidence, and continuous invisibility will also lead to less money. If people don't know you, or they are not confident about what you do, you are less likely to be a successful entrepreneur. You will find yourself in a constant process of feeling stuck because no one can see you.

I work with women entrepreneurs, but this person reached out to me because he was having some trouble. Let's say his name is Ted. Ted was having some trouble with his ability to be seen in his specific space. As we discussed it, it was not about what he thought it was. It ended up being he was visible to the wrong people.

He wanted to speak to students at high schools and elementary schools, but we realized that his audience and the people that he could really establish himself as an expert in front of were really business owners and managers and executives. He was talking to the wrong people. As soon as I was able to realize that his brand is not right or he is positioning himself in the wrong market. I realized that I really do know a lot about this field, I need to just push myself out there and make it happen.

So working with someone really helped me realize that I was actually good at what I was doing. In addition I was branding myself. Sometimes you are your first client. Once you are able to put yourself out there and build your brand you are usually your first success story.

You have to remember, I was a teacher and I knew I needed to do more but I was completely stuck. I was teaching a class at a very good institution and I knew that I had to step out of my comfort zone. I just had to do something else. I was afraid to let people know that I had ran out of my savings as an educator.

I had left my job. I had been gone for over a year. I had ran out of my savings. I knew that if I didn't move to the next step that I was going to be bankrupt.

That is the real story. If I didn't start positioning myself and doing it very quickly, I was in the process of running a very expensive hobby. My expensive hobby was keeping me broke. It was keeping me stuck. It was keeping me frustrated and very annoyed. Because I knew that I was good and no one knew it. I knew that I could do this but no one could find me.

Why was this you ask? I was stuck because I wanted to lean so much on calling myself an educator that people did not know be as anything else. I had done so good of a job of branding myself as an educator. But I was insecure about branding myself as an entrepreneur.

I just had to go through the branding process again. I had to stop feeling bad for myself and understand that I was enough! Then my expensive hobby became who I was.

The 5 C's

Once you are able to go through that process of becoming a success for yourself, you can kind of figure out how to duplicate that for other people

So what are the things that you can do right now here today to be able to accelerate your profits, to brand yourself and to know that you are enough?

It starts with content, creation, connection, contribution and coaching. These are actually things that you do simultaneously.

Being a content expert means that you know your content and you let the world know that you know your content. Content is all about creating some ideas around your expertise

Creation is all about creating knowledge. Creating a product, a good or service. A program that can be out there in the world that people can join and learn from. Is you have a system that you put in place, it automatically puts you as an authority figure because you out yourself out there as someone who can create something. Not everyone can. You are a creator and not just a knower of knowledge.

Connection is us connecting with influencers, people who are experts that we can collaborate with and more than anything else, people can say,

"I saw that person with so and so." A perfect example of that would be Oprah. How many people do we believe in because they were on the Oprah show? I mean Dr. Phil is Dr. Phil now because of what he did on the Oprah Show. Dr. Oz is now Dr. Oz because we saw him on the Oprah show. Now they are experts in their own field, but it was who they were seen with that made that connection for their customers about them.

With social media, online networking has become extremely easy. You position yourself as the expert you are.

Experts know other experts. Connecting and collaborating with other influencers can really expedite your expertise. It can accelerate your expertise because you being seen with them. They are an expert and your name is being associated with them. At the same time it's also pushing you up there as an expert.

You don't have to worry about competition. I don't worry about competition because I truly do believe in collaboration. And when you connect with other influencers you bring some valuable information to the table in a different perspective

Contribution is simply us adding value to the community; social media, on our blog, on other people's posts. We are making tweets, periscopes, all of those kind of things that are contributing worthwhile information out into the world. You want to contribute to the social media conversation, and have a social media presence. Not just for the sake of having it, but to contribute value

And then lastly, coaching. We need to invest in a coach that has already done what we want to do so that there is somebody that can help us avoid pitfalls and give us information on how to be able to take the best path from here to there.

These are the five C's of accelerating your expertise. If you do these five C's, you will expedite your expertise. You will accelerate your profitability, visibility. Being heard, being seen and being paid.

This is something that you can do today. You can identify even one small thing that you know you know and then let tell the world you know it. You can make even the simplest of systems available for people to use. You can find an expert in your field and start thinking about a collaboration. You can send out a tweet or a write a blog post today that adds value. You can seek out information from a coach who has established themselves as an expert.

You don't need to wait you can do this now!

When you step out on faith. When you start to do all five C's. Then you can know **You Are Enough**. And as we do we will find that our branding has helped us accelerate our expertise and our profit.